CICADA

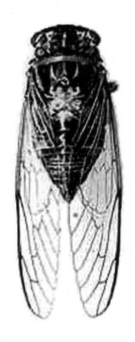

MARK NICKELS

RATTAPALLAX PRESS

Rattapallax Press

532 La Guardia Place
Suite 353
New York, NY 10012

website: www.rattapallax.com

Ram Devineni, *Publisher*

Printed in the United States of America.

ISBN: 1-892494-22-1 (paperback)
ISBN: 1-892494-23-X (E-book)
LCCN: 00-104014

For
Kenneth Paul Nickels
(1946-1994)

Grateful acknowledgement is made to the following, who, in whatever capacity, have made a contribution to this book in its present form:

David Brinkerhoff, George Dickerson, Tanya Goetz, Maureen Holm, Jo-Ellen Kwiatek, Donna Munro, Chuck Nickels, Sally Norvell, William Pitt-Root, M.A. Schaffner, Larissa Shmailo, Victoria Tilney, Louis Villaire, Judith Werner, Eric Yost, Michael T. Young and Steffen Zellinger.

To those countless not mentioned who have added to the richness of the narrative, both told and untold, and allowed me to play some part in theirs, to my poor thanks I append these poems.

These poems, some in different versions, have appeared or are forthcoming in the following publications:

"Cemetery" and portions of other poems in this volume appeared in the chapbook *Pages from the Summerland* published in 1991 by International Review Press and edited by publisher Louis Villaire and Donna Munro.

"Letter from Arthur" appeared in the *Asylum Annual*, 1993. In 1997, it was awarded first prize in the Milton Dorfman Poetry Competition judged by Jo-Ellen Kwiatek.

"Waterfall Effect" and "This Kindled by Gaude Virgo Salutata" appeared in *Rattapallax, No. 1* (February 1999), and were nominated by the magazine for the annual Pushcart Prize.

"Shells" and "Virgil'd" appeared in *Rattapallax, No. 2* (September 1999) and *No. 3* (March 2000).

"Mrs. Onassis is Spying on Patrons in the Temple of Dendur" appeared in *Medicinal Purposes Literary Review* (September 1999).

"Fell Summer" appeared in *Rattapallax, No. 4* (September 2000).

CONTENTS

AN OLD NEW LIFE

This will be better, the life after the life,
in another time, among the essences.
He will sacrifice the analogues of fire,
the neon fires, blue cathode fires. Then
he'll know, not the smell of something burning,
but the agitated, firstborn fire itself.
Over any torn meadow, the sun revolves
to coax speared wheat with a measured word.
Iron will mimic bone, but no one will be fooled,
the marrow teaches without question.
A kiss will be a cloth that barely conceals,
spread over the face of her body. It will
mislay her grimness suddenly, a smile
beneath the folds. But this is now.
A wraith loiters by his spine in tired clothes,
envying the dead their finish, though avid
for more living. There is a daily tomb
of Tuesdays and Thursdays, delved in February's name,
a name too thin to feed on,
and in fluorescent fade-light, rayed from nowhere,
his living holds its breath and waits for what has passed.

SAUDADE

I am so lonesome.
I am the last man in the world.
I tried forgetting you, but you've still been on my mind.

Come back the triceratops, double-hided and cross!
Come back Buonaparte, the little corporal
and we miss you, Savanarola!
Come back P.T. Barnum, the Romanesque, the battle of Cross Keys,
the tambour and the rebec and the bagpipe!

Marinetti, Mr. Ed, I wrote down all the funny things you said.

Come back Lola Montez, Virginia Woolf; come back Tin-Tin,
come back fan-dancing, fiddlesticks, the Venerable Bede,
the Commedia del Arte, Elenora Duse, and hobby horses!
What Time is it Mr. Fox?

I could watch a public hanging, and not look away.
I wish someone would call me, then put me on hold.
Come back Lloyd George and Oliver Cromwell, D'Annunzio,
Boy George and Georgie Goebel; Ma and Pa Kettle, Ma Barker,
Ma Rainey and Malraux!

Fame is the sunshine of the dead, said Balzac.

Come back the Golden Hind and courtly manners.
I want sodomy and gomorrahmy, that I never tried—
witch trials, witch hazel and cornbread.
Feed me roast pork and porridge and lima beans,
then I'll jump a burning pyre, jump a hurdle,
play bocchi and ride a unicycle, a bull. Let me race you!

You're it! You're the one! You're the one for me!
You're a ball buster. You slay me, you crack me up.
Let's sing: *Roll Out the Barrel, How Wonderful the Matchless Grace
of Jesus, the Pearlfishers Duet, Get Your Big Ol' Leg Offa Me.*

Give me dense, black, loamy slices of dreamless sleep
entwined with somebody else.
Tell me your secrets.
Why were you standing in the garage
with a forked divining rod just to the left of the oil spill?

Make me a tomato sandwich.
Put on band-aid, I skinned my knee.
It's starting to rain.
Pass me the kaleidoscope, please.

Scenes from childhood.
When we went to my Aunt's house,
the smell of frying bluegills from Little Green Lake misted the house.
My father sautéed the pink eggs along side the fish
and made his specialty, wilted lettuce, with bacon grease and
vinegar. My Aunt offered us spanish peanuts from a tupperware container,
and put salt in her beer. She looked quite a lot like Martha Raye.

I miss you Louisa May Alcott, Amelia Earheart, Alger Hiss!
I remember your eyes, Edward Plantagenet, bloodshot
when you were vexed. I remember your pearl earring
Charles the First, stepping over the casement at Whitehall.

Dewey beats Truman, hearts trump spades, Kennedy beats Nixon,
le roi has been captured at Poitiers!
My parents said *don't play with the fire, you'll wet the bed.*
Good Night and God Bless, said Red Skelton.

Come back Acteon, who should have looked away,
and Neville Chamberlain, who did.
Come back Li Po and Lao-tse and Lorca!
Come back Jubal Early and John Clare and Christopher Smart,
Justice Learned Hand, Berlioz, DeQuincy and Cocteau!

I fondly dream of plague, diphtheria and smallpox,
and moaning in the night.
God Bless Thee Friend I would go to Quaker meeting and sit low.
I want to chop wood and take out the trash,
bind some twigs and vacuum the rug.
Peer over the palings:
I'll be hanging out the washing on the Siegfried line.
When that's done I'll even wipe down the credenza, for chrissakes!

Bring hot water, bring the kids, bring out your dead
that won't stay buried anyhow, and who run our world.
I'd like some dead to bury, if nothing else.

My whole life, this peculiar *saudade.*

THE WATERFALL EFFECT

Three is a number which, if you rotate it slightly
to the left, spills a cascade of oranges and loam
from its stacked cups in a short fragrant river,
like a lifetime shocked daily by beauty:
down the steps the gold nova harborwise,
the dank, biophilic smell of the sea.

Molten, shattering, passed leaf to leaf,
the shuttle of dayend in July, one of the moments
stored in a bright file of summers,
to be unpacked, maybe, at extreme unction.
Yes, to salt away sublimity that way,
in pungent sheaves, a pressing of the scent
of wet trees with the sound of crows and waves,
storing it in a vault, and when one opens it,
to have the instant wafting out: the trees
that waved breathing in woodwinds,
the wind in violins, the highborn air
cold, cold and aloft in horns.

I imagine all this stored in the trinitarian number
in layers of heat and cold, cartilage and smoothness.
The oranges are a refinement of everything the dirt knows.
A poem is the lay of the marrow and minute electricity,
a conduit of the day's phenomena, to wit, the invasion
of the palmetto bugs and the nautical sea-shanty sound
of some of Bartok's themes (astonishing Hungarian lovelies
though they may be), the jets of braided water,
the voices, the voices pressed and tumbling in
Josquin des Prez, the waterfall effect.
How I played a Bruckner symphony, and the neighbors

upstairs played *A Whiter Shade of Pale*, and the two
in the same key contrapuntally merged into something new.
And the bassoon, the bassoon in a Victoria Mass
sounds to tonally orient the choir, and at that moment,
a foghorn in the harbor plays the identical note.

All this in a poem.
Among other things, a poem.

A poem is the record of the way the world rhymes with itself.

And for the eyes, the folding, the fervid skiagraphia
of leaves, of leaves and buildings in New York,
the interplay between the brick and the sycamore, arcing.
I feel the forest in Brooklyn, I hear the footfalls
of a primal ghost, and in the last week of July
the cicadas are again coming in concealed heraldry,
green-star flags in the plane trees,
scarabs on the spines of books, the annals of rain inside.
Sacred, they complete the circle of a place.
How a moment sounds the same over time,
their atavistic rasping a disdain for time.
The river rises and falls, and human beings
pass under, mere shades, a blur, a trembling
in the surface of the air, and Cassiopeia wheels,
and Cassiopeia wheels, she wheels morningward always.

SKELETON

Descend into the skeleton, noting all the deep
structures like leaves, the unlikely photographs.
Yes, I have portals and stalls to walk through,
nocturnal films, and you, meandering the estate
of someone long absent, and here you are welcome.
Slide in your stocking feet on the slippery oak,
the long gallery, make use of the clotheslines,
the acres of linen that cover the chairs,
the cupboards stuffed with useless green felt,
the coffee urns. Beware of the west wing:
the gaps between the slatted floors,
the unstable lathing on the walls, the drop-off.
From all of this time spent, will it be possible
in your skeleton or mine, to construct a narrative,
the painfully untold, also the merely untold,
the long film that disintegrates with time,
the question of its distinctiveness unasked.
Through different filters we see
wavering New York, large canyons of mind
strangely russet, and is a portion of our mind
rented permanently by a huge collective
in which language and history are bylaws?
So sweet to imagine my mind not my property,
not making me feel powerless, but grandly gifted,
entrusted with the estate of someone long absent.
And where is he walking, on a medieval covered
bridge, his hands, his hands on his hips
overlooking a piazza, pigeons wheeling
in the shapes of the alphabet, turning in the red air,
crossing a dry stream floored with oak leaves;
a cave in India where bats unfurl like umbrellas

and swoop into the darkness? The house is empty,
the owner is away, who shines his headlight
in other caves, a glistening of water
down a smooth rock; who is fishing for bluegills,
watching his bobber recede in the dusk
while keeping the top of his head cool,
drinking water from caves deep under France.
He is watching a young woman, a young woman
from Mexico sunbathing on a roof, a young
woman from Mexico. When he returns to us,
inside him this bone armor (Rosalinde the skeleton)
he will reacquaint us with this painful grandeur.
We will be content and will have had the time
to survey the yard, gather the leaves with rakes,
and finally, just prior to darkfall, set fire to the piles.

SHELLS

Essentially, for some time, in an effort
to determine whether I loved you or not,
I've been praying to you, even though
the inside of the tabernacle, as I thought,
is empty: oxygen, carbon dioxide,
brass, nickel, and a sheet, a sheet
of gilded plywood. (And in the rectory,
the housekeeper is cooking pasta, stamped
in the shape of shells, all of a uniform size
and color.) In an effort to determine,
in an effort to determine whether I loved you,
whether I loved you or not,
I learned old lovers are christs or bodhisattvas.
Slowly at first, and then with greater skill,
in an effort to determine whether I loved you,
I loved you or not,
I've been praying without knowing it,
in the daylight, in the white afternoon,
and singing, and singing with records,
my head tilted up into the black walnut,
the windows alive with listening ravens
to whom I sing about your boxy feet
with rind of callus at the heel,
(as elsewhere noted), your smiting eyes,
your nose pugged slightly, like Socrates,
your dark skin, your dark.
Your voice like a woodwind, a basset clarinet;
the wind you went out on, the wind you came in on,
your hair the color of a violin,
the unambiguous quality of many of your pronouncements,
i.e., the time you said I was tortured by life,

your eyes boring through me, right
for the wrong reasons, again.
The time in New Orleans you were so angry,
I was so drunk, lurching in the curio shops full of shells.
A shell grows around itself, folding over
the first pattern, calcified into a whorled shape, not dissimilar
to the whorl on the top of our two heads,
the pattern of gorgeous irreplaceable error,
and for a while the only assurance we belonged,
we belonged to the same species.
And the joy was piercing, this piercing joy
came up in me, a whirring train, night,
on the way home, somewhere before Memphis.
The singing in my ears. A hurricane,
a hurricane outside to my right was photographed from a satellite
even as a criminal was being printed,
his thumb whorl down, twisted clockwise,
and the trees out in the dark strained,
growing, forming knots, their flesh burled in the timedrift.
I've wondered: does the twisting hurt them,
and did all your turnings and hidings wound you
as they did me, and did you notice my imprint,
my concealment in that fold of air beside you,
when into your boxy feet and brown hands
nails, nails were driven,
when you got into that car and went west,
when you sat under that tree almost forever?

A Long and Swerving Conch

The surfaces romance me. When the salt trucks rain in the street, the cars roll over the unbroken pellets with a hollow fricative, hailstones on a cathedral roof. Elsewhere, like a consort of viols inside, the morning wheezes somberly awake. A clean shirt I'm unfolding has a tearing sound I like, not adhering to itself. I am ready for what? To see more, it looks like, and, thankfully, though there's no money in it, hear more. I notice the phenomenal world observes all the repeats. Are the workday combinations different from yesterday, or was I not paying attention? I was screening films in the frontal lobe, no doubt, about unfulfilled particulars. I noticed they'd only lose about thirty seats if they put an aisle down the middle.

Though not exactly rested, see how my black and loamy wedge of sleep, just now digitally truncated, rhymes with the following: Schubert's *Unfinished* in my north-lit room. This old seahorse and the Sonata d. 960: written by someone with inside information about their own mortality.

A French historian theorizes that up until a couple of hundred years ago people knew when they were going to die, days, months in advance, and prepared quietly for same. This skill has faded, a lovely green signal, dashboard-colored, no longer rising above the press of microwaves. Myself, I have noticed fewer and fewer déjà-vu episodes as I've gotten older. The music is draped this morning in its brooding snow-cloud get-up, led by a conductor untimely killed in a bathing accident. Note the overlays: my truncated sleep, the *Unfinished,* the young morto-conductor whose baton may still be heard. These overlays can become very fine, with attention. Every day, I tell you, like stepping up to the lip of a long and swerving conch, and going in. I am embedded in what I see the way the bird I heard when I opened my eyes just now was embedded in jet wheeze—a jet, a great winking abomination, but also a room with seated people in it. They are stretching, looking out at gothic Manhattan, a city with *jongleurs* but no wolves.

I read *The Diary of Samuel Pepys* on the subway, how he supp'd last night on boiled milk and a pullet, then stopped to get his periwig rehaired and dusted, a cone over his face like a wind-up fox. His domicile is a mess, he says, with cheese laying about, but life gets done. At that London instant, my old neighborhood, the one I grew up in in Michigan, is still a rocking wood-lot where poplars flip us their gleaming undersides with great tenderness, though there are brambles that can trip you.

I'll take it, even if, as the Buddha says, it is impermanent, *not-Self,* unsatisfactory. I'll take it, sleepy, and with the feeling—which I won't be deprived of—that it matters about as much as I think it does, and it's my hand that makes the adjustment, cranking up or down the significance of the moment like Simon Bar Sinister.

And I've got to find a little danger somewhere, to leverage the relative safety of this life against three million years of running after cross and dangerous potential meals, the fear of having my skull staved in in my sleep, the sparkling marrow inside probed with sooty fingers while they hold me down. I remember that, and wake up screaming. I remember rhythmically trundling along that railroad handcar too (ah, the rhythm of love), escaping the police, opening and closing drawers in that deserted farmhouse, looking for things. It wasn't me, but it *was*, and outside gongs shuddered in the wheat, bronzing everything.

Dreams are like bleeding radio waves from other people's lives, a log-jam of whole, discrete instants, a vast, pointillist canvas, and we never get over them, the others, and we are never alone. But dreams aside, conditions, the way things are, actuality—all our fights about it (mostly with ourselves) have a certain rank poignancy, like rancid lavender, or backed-up crying, a smell like ammonia rearing in the sinus cavity—a billowing, x-ray shroud.

Perform this exercise. It is only Thursday, but imagine yourself away from the earth so long that when you finally get back and get in the door, and go through the mail, everything you hated while here is new again, and blameless. Your nose runs and your eyes tear, though it could be the wind.

You are hungry, and not overly concerned. All the epochs of the spot you're standing in surround you, right here, shuttling by, a book of days fanned close to your face. You breathe, your lungs as impersonal as the lowering stratocumulus, the bellows mechanism without patent anywhere. Your movements, and those of your friends, are plotted on the spine. This much is plain: one thing in this blurred schematic, so delicious, is not much larger or of greater duration than another, because it all transpires against a stillness unimaginably dense, an emptiness empty even of emptiness, and for our purposes, forever.

FIRECRAFT

July 4th, 1999, New York City

How rich you are, an urchin said to Wilde,
advancing under Covent Garden with
a bank of orange lilies. And as the 20th ends,
in the city indisputably its capital,
I gasp the same. Fireworks. Before the finish,
they send a drift of willows up, massive,
coppery, lazy in their fall, the towers
all but hidden by these ember trees.
The least of circuses are consequential.
If less so than bread, one may feed
on the polity's undirectional love.

On the other roof, camcorder monitors
are cool and blue, the operators slender
in their shorts, well cared for, with all
their vaccinations, their eyes the color
that they chose. The bursts have panicked
car alarms, which wobble like an alien invasion
in a Fifties movie. And interesting
the continuities: the same saltpeter smell
as when the headlines shouted *French Guns
Open Up!*–those flashes could be coming
from the Somme. The braying tugs
could well be hooting on the Thames,
VE day, or like an oboe in an Overture, Rameau.

Yesterday, we staggered in a heat wave,
Virgil, June and I, to a museum, where
a 3D video of Nippon goddesses unfolded.
Virgil vaguely watched, an infant, his eyes
a lens unfocused, while I stood behind

and tried to fit the glasses to his head.
I must have wanted to amaze, transfix him,
insure that there was nothing he would miss.
And then I knew I 'd forego none of this:
the whole as futuristic as I could have
wished for, nine or ten, and guessing
what the streaming future would be like.

My computer, with a banner, just
suggested, *Looks like you're trying
to write a letter? Can I help?*
But I'm *not,* or *am* I, Virgil?
You are sixth months old now, frowning
and Churchillian. When you read this
I may be dead, or frozen in the moon.
It is 1999, and I always
write in light now. Our wars are *surgical,*
though as random and ham-handed
as they always were. The circuses are instant
and marvelous to point of dread, but tonight
the same as when the Chinese Emperor
had charges packed with gold, so that from barges,
his minister of firecraft could incise
these willows on the inky sky.
I'm not an urchin, nor will you be. No one
is overawed forever. See how in planes,
the passengers will draw the shade, while outside,
inside sleeves of cloud, every expectation
they ever held of heaven. Sublimity
is never, maybe, what this mammal wanted.
Even if it lost itself in images forever,
legs folded on the bank, there would still be pain,
the crossed sciatic spears in back and legs
from shaking out the rice all day,
or from shaking out these letters, still
the only food that keeps us ravening for life.

THE TWENTIETH CENTURY

We had the new Chevrolet steel Idyll, sky-blue metal with the salmon interior, *A Sunset On Wheels*.

We had silver moving clowns, the most famous of which resembled our worst villain, which confused us. Little toothbrush mustaches.

We had an abundance, for once, of chocolate and tobacco, and nearly everyone drank a sweet bubbly beverage flavored by a South American plant. It somewhat burned our nose and throat.

My mood was sweet and even, the rain was warm driving down the road with the radio on. It played some lovely exciting tune. Then, an unctuous voice with news of war.

You drove to work with your coffee between your legs, the line ahead pink near the tree line, your dashboard with serene green lights. In the back seat was a Wild Bill Hickock coloring book and a small sneaker. It said *Red Ball Jets*.

You stumbled into the cold green sea, enervated, with a dry mouth, afraid you might step in a hole and drown. You can't swim. The beach is ahead, some palm fronds wave. It's beautiful, like Bali Hai, but there are planes descending *ack ack ack*, making filmic little fountains of sand where they strafe the beach. Finally, reaching the woods, and separated from your company, you fall asleep.

Some of your son's crayons melted in the back window. Remember to scrape those up, or melt it with wax paper and an iron, as the newspaper instructed.

Bring home the Butternut Bread, Fred.

We each had Rangoon Night Market Noodles. They were salty, with pieces of duck. Then we went to a movie. Someone sat on my homburg. When it was over, we walked out stunned and embarrassed. Even mediocre films communicate with one's childhood. The line of people waiting to get in examined us carefully. And for an hour after this, every little sound was delicious: the keys in our pocket, the creak of our seats, the bedsprings when we crawled into bed, effects in a soundtrack. Our sex was a little melodramatic, with a loopy grandeur. And afterwards we were *so* thirsty.

We watched the solar eclipse in Dad's welding helmet, his crusader's helm, wobbling and blind.

Our tongue always smarted with the astringent mint of the toothpaste when we moved to the bed, and she was always burning holes in her nylons with those goddamn Pell Mells.

Sunday night you were alone in the farmhouse, near sunset. It had been a hot day, with cicadas humming in the corn, the sound rising into the hot blue silver. You took a bath, and when you walked into the living room, still a little wet, the curtains planed horizontal, and you could hear distant thunder. The radio was low, playing classical music. The corn leaves were active, but discreet. That night you sat on the front porch steps drinking your son's Hi-C citrus cooler. A special events floodlight examined the horizon.

Under a sky thick and like pewter, lying there reading with the window open, you heard a Brooklyn catbird imitate a car alarm, the series of warbles and chirps identical, and in the same sequence. The famous Car Alarm Bird.

You like the way the brushes sound over the car radio when the drummer plays with a small ensemble. As the station gets further away, the sound of the brushes mixes with static, as though some small bright particles were bunched there at the end of his hands. You worry about the car when you leave the tarmac because the bottom pings with small stones from the hardpan. The red radio towers blink far ahead, and off to the right. Soon you move up under them.

ANIMALIA

Double tusks thrust up toward Canis Major,
the woolly mammoth folded in the earth
was seen to shudder vertical, via satellite,
his eyes dust-filmed, his hide in leathery folds,
but angry, charging cameramen and cars,
a cyclone on the interstate.

The tree frogs made us stupid, we fled in our pajamas,
the yellow road in dim disquiet, the insects siren-loud.
The medians, they writhed, a mania of fur.
We climbed a slope, our home hills brushing by us,
running through the woods to the radio tower.

We were running through the woods and climbed the hill
and there we encountered refugees in sportswear,
who told us how lost brooks beneath the town
smashed up through broken pavement, the hives beneath collapsed.
The koi in fishponds churned until the churning made a sound,
and truly Fear stormed up the neural stairs
and took the upper mammal brain, which mostly packed it in.
Only schizophrenics weren't surprised,
who were attentive to the ailanthus as it crackled
in its manic growth like Vincent's writhing cypresses,
who heard the snidely catbird mimicking a car alarm,
who know the planet will be shrugging off its toxins when we're gone,
the earth absurdly old. And if it takes
a hundred thousand years, or five times older
than the written word—in deepest time, it doesn't signify.

Some of these were heard to laugh when fangs
sank into throat and ass: how the awful grace

concealed in whirlwinds and in floods
could lunge at you behind the dumpsters,
and all this while you fumbled with your keys.

Now we walk museums with no roof,
sodden dioramas and stained walls.

When Rome went down, the Visigoths
cut off the pricks and noses on the statues
of the vanquished. Now animals pluck out
the marble eyes of taxidermied brethren,
offended by the useless stones we put there,
dull, with no reflectors in the back of them.
And so our eyeless friends, our charges,
glare vacant at us. We thought they were
companions in destruction; we were ticking off
extinctions with a dank regret. Now,
we avoid their places, as they avoided ours.

O now they lurk in war, plunging
through the strip malls, surging
through the tumbling aisles of house wares.

There is a bat-house in a tollbooth on the turnpike,
and they hang from bones there. On an island.
Where the river took the road.

TIGER LILIES

Like Houdini from my selfhood, how
I slipped the knot without intending to,
and seventeen, against a sun-baked garage,
merged into aisles of tiger lilies, toppling,
giddy with their flaming top weight.
I came from school and filched a glass of red,
and drank it quick, and moping through our yard
sat down there, feeling loose, peculiar,
pointed where the golden, standard Tuesday
stalled behind the water tower, Fisher Body.
(The garage—depression brick, a shingled tar,
a nap you tore off in the summer meltdown,
and that rendered middle-western bungalows
distantly like cardboard packing boxes,
though closer, complicated, shot with mica.)
The microwaves or whatnot tumbled
in a flaming ring, the evening newsmen level
under static, their voices through the railroad cuts
all southerly away, haunting empty playgrounds.
I think they put your dinner on, that instant,
and they called you.
                     Just then, not a thing
not me: not boulders, lilies, or the blackbirds
plashing in the neighbor lady's birdbath,
birds not owned by anyone, the way
I cannot own my breath, this soft and shunned
arrhythmia, a handsaw borrowed for this turning.
Much like the hotdog joke: someone
going to the vendor in the park
and asking him to *make me one with everything*—
like being on the inside looking out, for once,

not on the outside looking in. Maybe
this I couldn't know then, and perhaps
I don't know now. And then it stopped.
I got inside the house and played a record,
Debussy, I guess, the *Faun,* the closest
I could come, and tried to hold
the feeling just then winking out with yet
another glass, and then another after that.

HAUNTS

One day, in Fall, a toxin entered into me.
I expelled it then, but not before an impress.
I sidestepped, shuddered, froze and turned
into a scarab, avoided looking in the mirror,
but shaved by touch, and shaved my head.
Altogether I became a sliver, a shutter,
a shadow in the Prado, a maneuver
to become someone about whom nothing was known.
I fished, made inexpensive meals for myself,
and recorded on a tape broods of cicadas,
wastrels, new-shelled layabouts with husks,
eternal loafers, like the dead, at once
companionable, and disinterested.
Thinking of the people I had met that day
with love and fear, and up all night
to welter in the wake and by the haunt of others,
I reckoned the whole thing a haunt:
my brain, the world, the diorama clouds,
somehow love's hardware damaged,
a signal curse of watchers and of waiters
passed in the blood of bitter ancestors,
a fold in air I delved out for myself,
an envelope to shelter in.

When my father, lowered by a winch into the ground,
was lowered by a winch into the ground,
the others in the family clustered while I stood apart
and dealt myself this little wound.
At least it has not worsened over time.
By indirection I survey dimensions of this spell
of otherness, the sourceless grief, the volume

of the violence there, self-loathing in a short parade
that trails me with its panoply of fireworks,
a train of invisible pull-toys clicking, and whirring.
I hardly see it anymore, a festival creche
for my Brooklyn fire ants. Still,
when good things happen, look into my ear:
two creatures in the mind still slash and bite each other.
But I have weighed these things, and now
I work. It is what happiness costs.

LETTER FROM ARTHUR

Well, Lance, last night Gwen and I monitored the lunar eclipse
to make certain nothing untoward happened. It's a peaceful
morning. Gwen is off somewhere, and the cat is surfing across
the dining room floor on sheets of scratch paper. I'm leaning
on the battlement dropping pieces of toast into the albumen—
silver process of the moat in which the trees glower as darkly
as ever. Ha!

Do you remember when that maiden came from the woods and
stayed just long enough to tell you you were no longer the number
one flower of chivalry? And that, as they say, was that. Then
you went off and chased that tired griffin through the high summer
mines. Sometimes you could hear it ahead of you in the shaft, padding
softly, with the slightest crunching. At other times, it wheeled
around in the dark behind you, or turned the corner, suddenly.
The red moon grinned through the gratings. You could smell the
wind. You could hear the ladders of the hot leaves chafing together.
We found you waist high in a mirage, and I had the whole
court leave their lawn darts and slap you gently, one at a time,
until you came to, the mirage dropping around your knees.
People are vast.

Not long after, the Grail floated through the window, hard upon
us, a sort of metaphysical chafing dish. I asked you, *what will you
have? A French dip sandwich, the breaded shrimp plate, haricot beans and
squash, fish sticks and blue moon ice cream topped with Slim Jim's?*
This was not a mirage. Too many choices. Not like the old days
when we were happy with what we could get.

After you ate, all you knights got up and left us, farting. You
headed out on highway 80, looking for the Grail glimmering somewhere

above the aluminum savanna. Laughing your chesty laugh. You
stout knights, clinking like a grocery bag full of empties! Mocking, owing,
glowing, going away, your bright horn sounding through the pines.

Lift the Latch

I put my hands to it, those bottles
and attendant grandiosity, both as to a
warming fire, then burnt the house.
I'm tumbling to good, I guess, in
Brooklyn, on the vaunted middle path
where pennons do not, as a rule, snap
and plane level, nor do horns blare.

Listen. There is a furtherance in
communion I ignored, in which a hundred
hands as newly small as mine
have sistered in some beams, slow like,
a little at a time:
a place to stand, a place to sleep,
a place to put a table. And something else:
a heat and pressure gathering
like that in trees, so slow it isn't understood
as heat and pressure.

Maybe the willingness to lift the latch
for some coppery old god, from his cloak
the smell of the sea, of ponds, of ponds
and of saltgrass, of willows.
He spits on mottled birchbark
to build swallows, new and shrill,
rising from his cooling firepit,
rising from the copse in vortices,
in vortices and chatter.

And then,
and then in the middle of the night,
in a blue wind studded with fireflies,
he is wheeling through the yards on the way to the widow,
the widow
and her drunken son, because
he is like them, and emptiness,
emptiness anywhere
makes him intemperate,
like a drunk.
Only needless, not needful,
secure in abandon,
in making, and in filling up.

FALLEN SKY

The leaves are sere, and conceal the summer
rolled there, sweet ghosts of heat released
inside the brittleness. The cold pavilion
arcing over Brooklyn, chrome and emptied,
is whanging like a bell. As the branches bare,
all distances advancing, anguished, are a cortege
approaching nearer with their hats off.
If not anguished, everything you see, even
courageous bleached-sail cumulous, is only
template, a diorama fitted on an endless space.

Puddles. Windows. The shiny car. The earth
a hive of looking glass that won't reveal you.
There are maybe fourteen clues, compiled,
that you may use to locate you, but they
only work in order, all at once. Or maybe it is
that any *one* could open you, at intervals
to yourself. Maybe you are in this instant,
seconds after pain, between the gesture
to survive annihilating panic and the knowledge
that you have, puffing down the Promenade,
bitter after endless nights awake, your mind
missing like an old car, pursuing herds of ibex
as they vanish behind Borough Hall.
In the aftermath of seeing what you fear,
maybe this is who you are, and you are vertical
and scared, your face resembling childhood now,
all its gathered density, at last.
But don't pretend the moment changes you
forever. There is no forever here, but only sky,
which every day misplaces nothing of itself.

ANCESTOR WORSHIP,
DRIVING AT THE EDGE OF LAKE MICHIGAN

This is a cul-de-sac obsession, a search
for unearned value, an excuse.
But my eyes are turned this angle in my face
and what I'm seeing washes in in waves
to animate small hands, and flood a narrow head.
Did you stare down at your splayed toes in the dawn
while peeing, and wonder what just happened?
Did you scatter an old bum's bender of pocket change
around the floor, and leave your sleeves
unbuttoned and unrolled, or am I uniquely careless?

I reckon I'll go down to Hart. The subject,
reckless freedom, selling off the spuds,
another tavern slide, one final nickel on the zinc.
Then you're veering with the horses in the dark.
On your left, the molten moon dissolves
into the Lake. Once home, a woman draped
in black, severe but not reproachful,
lowers you to bed.

My own desires, my own. I do not need
a through-going push in one direction,
but there, a surge, and there, a pulling back,
a rail-walk between the unappealing and the less so,
the unknown. But we both will put our heads down, yes,
I reckon we will go. Go on. Some more.

We're threading our car down through tiny,
sleeping towns long after dark, the erect ones,
in a blurred red-metal cloud. I say to no one,
or pass this question to your shade, soft-breathing

underneath the dash. What are we going to do?
I've heard the unborn envy us, for reasons
that remain unclear. The dead dismiss us
from old newsreels with a waving hand
into the camera lens, grousing in a soup line,
or flagging down the paper-boy for news.
I drink green underground French water,
for I'm learning to be careful, sober,
driving fast, and with my other hand
guiding distant voices down green radio dials,
bright numbered halls where people murmur things
that don't make sense right now.
No one knows a thing.
And driving deaf and blind I have forgotten
where we are. The single streetlight
changes for no one, changes for you and I alone,
keeps us from collision with no one.

CANCER

My landlord cut a ring around the backyard tree,
and when the ring is joined, it dies. Then I looked
at Edward Curtis photographs, these Indians
in horns. On the whole, my Churchill minute
was brief, by the egg timer. Where the ape god lived,
the big noun supplanted by flocking unknown verbs,
is storage, also Eros. Five minutes today.
All by my lonesome. The Eternal Rehearsal.
Then I convened a rally with recorded bagpipes,
the neighbors raveling, unraveling their blankets.
Still, I am too civilized for this.
I need a headdress, horns and feathers, red ash
on my cheekbones, and bits of femur, laced with thong,
not a thin wail levitating, useless, into branches.
My sister should wear a rack of antlers, howl
at her daughter's bedside, breathing smoke
and fan it with a starling's tail. We're too gentle,
we've too much faith in modern fecklessness,
and I can't raise a curse. Unseen animals
divide in twos, then into four, then into eight,
you cannot flush them, like grouse, from thickets of lymph.
They are a mound of ghost ants: you kill them
by doing yourself in, like jumping off a cliff
when swarmed by deerflies. Or, like my niece,
they put you in a clean room, because you are defenseless.
If only, as in poems, we gained fluidity
by excision, or expansion. But these
are the spells of making, not retrievable for life.
I'd hover to the clean room of my niece,
joined by the others, one by one, the family,
the faces that, of all known faces, I instantly recall.

We'd herd there under horns, like the animals
we forgot we are, but looking arch, tender, fatigued.

THE LAST GLISSADE

c.2039 Astronomers postulate a near miss by a giant asteroid in this year.
A foreshadowing, for Lou

Old men, like boys of six, are absolutely
thorough, and button their top buttons.
At dusk, the oak and cottonwood go black
against the blue empire of night.
Neutrinos pierce us more and more, Sebastians
universal, and a blinking loon
is rising from the swamp. On the porch
I revolve your daughter to settle a dispute:
does she favor the distaff or the spear side?
And this though I can barely see the table
checkered blue, a glass of tea, the tiny box
that spills Dvorak's *Seventh Symphony,*
the personnel long since replaced, or dead,
the conductor and the lady on bassoon.

Old men confabulate in lawn chairs,
are then transported in electric trucks,
hats in their laps, passing the barefoot
in the gravel road, largely motionless and stoic.
Our speech seems discontinuous to others.
The pauses are discretionary—one waits
on the effect the latest repetition
of a name has on the other, maybe
a name without an owner anymore.

No one wants two elderly canoeing,
but we heckle some unfortunate to guide us,
elbone, armpit, one on either side,
down through the blowing fescue to the dock.
One more glissade on pond glass,

the only sound of oar-dip, and the rasp
of summer insects. We glide inside the lilies
where it mists, begin to fumble, wheezing,
slow, with cotton and with snaps, the clicks,
soft thuds and fastnesses of clothes.

Then we commence to turtle, chin beards
pointing up, bellying fools for napping
in the lake. Old and dry and kind,
the stars have come to move, or is that
a winking grid of satellites that children
know the names of, as once they knew
Orion, Cassiopeia, the Bear?

On a bark and wire flotilla in the Lake
the Ottawa control the weather
and monitor the fanning mane of sparks.

A hundred other nights, the chill would have us
back in our soft clothes, but tonight
a ritual to contemplate survival,
our breathing and our rest below,
above, the trackless Unborn left behind.

CEMETERY

Do they ask after you when you are passing the red points of radio towers?

Do they ask after you under sunspots, in aisles of clean consumer goods?

Do they ask after you with magnetic tape entwining your fingers like the moss
in your forests?

Do they ask after you while your home hills brush by you,

Where huge cities loom behind you not locatable in space, a hologram,

people doubled and tripled with mirrors?

Do they ask if you are taking care, if you are exhausted?

Do they ask if you have seen the constellations wheel around before dawn,

scattering blood and sparks, skittering into the day road

like a cigarette from a speeding car?

Do they see the dread fall from your face now and then, while a dog barks, an

engine races, bats sleep with apples after all, and the sky is what it is,

concealing nothing, not a museum diorama crafted by unknown others?

Are you praying with a god, or without?

Threshing in this nerve garden alone or with someone else?

Touching the radio to make it bloom?

Are you mouthing behind the shower curtain, your own Imam at sunrise,

firing words like tracer bullets into the hide of an animal that is asleep?

In dreams do you grip snakes by the jaws and fling them into crowds?

Do you watch bullets glide by slowly in gunfights?

Have you eaten blind fish, erect walker?

Have you eaten blind fish, like so many ideas?

Can what you do not know paddle cool in your blood?

We ask you this, the ones you planted, seismic needles in the ground.

Our cool stone listening towers blink white and black

in the shadows of blown trees.

LUDLOW CAFÉ

A voluptuary of unknowing, I huddle
in a vast wool coat. I case the orange walls,
outwardly as arid as Claude Rains,
but inwardly a woolly cipher, an *arriviste*
at some Three Stooges banquet, dithering between
the forcemeat popovers or the cucumber sandwiches
and rolling peas on crackers.
Now tentative and troll-like,
I move as though my coat were stuffed with Hummels,
china dogs, all stolen.

These Soho boys and girls, long noses
and short hair, black leather and black tights,
I'm watching them,
the affectations they've assumed just recently,
their home life in the suburbs fast receding,
the surreptitious pot smoking, glass tabletops,
shag carpeting, individuation, fear and secret sex.
The ordinary smells.
Yes, I am aroused, like someone in the *Counterfeiters,*
the *other.*

Oh Christ I love love love you,
with your violin colored hair, the silly way
you blow the smoke straight up;
looks like the steam from your father's factory
cheerfully vaporizing in the cold, Arcadian air.

A DAMNED ROSE MOMENT

Something to farm besides your mind
is what you want, to avoid the stretch of pasture
where a burial took place, where stood
an oak someone was hung from.
Sleep your way out, then, feet forward,
floating through the window, the aroma of the
weekly lamb cooked by the Saracens downstairs
lighting your way through the flaking sycamores,
a taper, umber, of cardamom.
Your rooms are being painted.
Your ordinary furniture is on the fire escape,
flaming, the lambent bottoms of the chairs
like sacred flotsam pulled from a flood of slate.
You don't recognize your junk—or you.
You could be anyone, and probably are,
but far enough along to forego panic
when you can't find yourself. Your past
is a mass of intricate sound, a thousand
morning wood lots, just fainter than the noise
you're making, thinking, in your skin.

MRS. ONASSIS IS SPYING ON PATRONS
IN THE TEMPLE OF DENDUR

Mrs. Onassis looks at the museum with her telescope.

Home from the airport, she takes off her shades
and eats assorted greens, spiked like the rampion
by the rounded feet of saints in Flemish paintings.
Kindling the radio, there are concertos by Vivaldi,
the brown, the umber loneness of bassoons.
Her telescope awaits her, a gift of Templesman
the wise. To spy on those below reverses
her polarities, rhymes with the days
she wandered Washington as *Inquiring Camera Girl.*
She trains it on the Metropolitan below her,
the Temple of Dendur. It has a magick'd lens
with which she looks through walls and time.
Men living and men dead bourrée, brocaded,
in full view, and then recede. They rally at the plinth
behind the Met, where they put on horses clothes
and are ridden through the park.

A character in a room in that Museum, as it was in 18th century Venice.

A mock-up 18th c. Venetian room
has mirrors on the wall. Now, these mirrors want
resilvering, but in that room and on that day
I dipped a crust in runny yolk. Betimes the sun
exploded on the casements, signaling
the everyday ignition of the gold canals.
I rose and peed into a china pot,
the room invaded with the buttery smell.
Last night I had some cuttlefish in pastry shells,
some roasted meadowlarks, new wine.

Today, a little crowd of pimps and urchins
drift and hover, watch me sashay mirrorwards
with a rococo bounce before I shoo them out,
the offspring of domestics who extol
the virtues of their sisters with an undulating hand.
Outside, Hot Sister Venice, she both
dank and fair, a lovely ageless girl
pulled from the sea. I hear blue Zephyr
galing lust into the city, the stones like
piping loaves, the sun delving in canals.
How are you, Signore? the urchins ask.
I'm dying, how are you?—sweating blood into my silks,
shitting, drooling, spare, like a *gisant*.
A doctor, Viennese, is cupping me
and always whistling: basset whistling, low.
Welts surging on my flesh, like cafe-table rings,
Der Artzt uncorks a mincemeat of jarred leeches.

I'm dying. I'm in a lust for humankind,
and everything about them: their homely smells,
the secret places of their bodies.
In dreams I'm walking golden, stunned,
out of the picture, in a delirium for touch:
rind, not essence, the watcher who
remains obscured. Cold news billows
in my arteries.

Last night, undressing, I saw behind me
her, half curtained in the dark, in this gimcrack,
gilded gloom, a woman with black hair
who looked like Death in Cocteau's *Orpheus*
the one who said, when speaking of the gods,
they go on and on, like the wind in your forests,
like the tom-toms of your Africa.
She watches as I sleep.

In truth, she comes in every night
with *grosso* hair, in a Cassini winding sheet
with nubby weave, and I see it all
from up there by the gilding, as though
the whole tableau were happening for someone else.
And soundlessly we talk about the ghosts
entwined around our spines in tired clothes.
And we are older than anyone.

ASTOR PLACE OPERA HOUSE RIOT

In the year 1849, a massive crowd, at its core made of young men from Ireland, surrounded the Astor Place Opera house, a theater built by the wealthy aristocrats of the city of New York. Mostly of English descent, the "knobs" inside were hosting a performance by the English actor Charles Macready. He was appearing there as Macbeth, a role being assayed elsewhere in the city by another actor, the darling of the young Irish "b'hoys", Ned Forrest. The crowd attacked the theater, singing out lines from the play. Troops were alerted, and volleys were fired into the surrounding crowd, killing twenty-three. The location, near the Cooper Union, is now the site, among other things, of a specialty coffee franchise.

In 1849, there's still the brown smell of a living river
or the sea. I'm hearing musket fire on Astor Place, just downtown
from where Broadway goes awry: a distant, rending sheet

that hangs in piggy lanes, and empty lots with rocking fescue.
Blue cirrus day. The men in soap locks and high hats
have throaty chants, *when the hurly-burly's done,*

when the battle's lost and won, that dovetail nicely with the Celtic
need to lose. *Shakespeare is a Sligo name.* A stench of nitre
when the muskets loose a cloud, like a *Chinee* laundry.

Megan smiles and smokes, her mocha beading in a plastic cup.
She doesn't hear the wails and curses in the breezeway
of the coffee shop, and I'm a dot: gauzy, airborne, hovering,

insinuated in these creases in the air, and everything
that ever happened happens *now:* the curtained sunset fire
suspended in the street, the shying horses, the melon-colored stone.

Notes from Deux Montagnes, Quebec

There are always two crows on the fence rails,
or on the overpass, though if they tell us we're
getting warmer or cooler, I couldn't tell you.
And in the boneyards, names like gothic blooms,
or vines entwined on iron: *Arthur La Tulippe*
et son epouse, Fleurette Desjardins. Between the stone rows,
killdeer and yellow jackets: Merovingian bees,
like the ones Napoleon had sewn on his
coronation robes, pilfered antiquities.

All these are newly dead, *arrivistes* to the Silent Lands.
Elusive our three times *grandpere,* Simon Charron,
et son fils, Guillaume. Maybe the old grave markers,
made of the soft, yellow, riverine stone, have melted off
in this Laurentian bottomland, or the dead were
tossed out back on the trek to the southwest, the farm
sold to Telesphore Croteau, or Euclide Repentigny,
while the living smoked, and drifted into pines,
to Michigan, without a context, and in search of cold beer.
I walk the line between their outstretched feet.
The DNA faintly worries the dousing rod, but distantly,
distantly. Maybe our dead have been stacked so low,
here in St. Eustache, St. Hermas, St. Augustin,
the bones set so deeply in the lower tiers
of marled clothing, rotted pine and loam,
their voices cannot rise above white beards
that bank the empty sockets like a drift of cottonwood.
Snow in the dark. I last saw him, Napoleon Charron,
great-grandfather, in photographs, in black. Maybe
he has transmigrated into one of these crows, who,
with his short body and beaked nose,

he vaguely resembles. The chain of fried chicken
restaurants everywhere are called *St. Hubert,* the saint
who discovered deep frying by dropping his breviary
in a vat of bubbling cartwheel grease.
His only relics here are names and faces: thick brows,
the Normandy bill, bent from the forehead like a scythe.
The forest birches, in their teens, topple willy-nilly
as though drunk, the leaves they feed themselves with
like a swarm of eyes, too heavy for the pliant trunks.
A radio tower blinks, transmitting Yves Montand
to old women who smoke three fags a chanson.
The sleepy announcer humors them on the phone,
repeating *bon, bon, bon.* Behind the church in St. Hermas,
the alfalfa plains are greener than you've been given a right to expect,
the clouds like sterling bales rounding the skyline west,
a procession of ice-haired kings mounting the steps of the world.
The poplars applaud such slow, majestic turbulence,
much like the dead, disappearing in some sweet violence,
in some grave agitation: agitation on so vast a scale,
it appears to have stopped.

THIS IS OVER

1

You took yourselves outside for photographs
by curbs, on squares of grass, in places in America
when planes were out. Mornings, you saw only
contrail, and always sun like snow, blurring
the creased faces, tail-fins, spare tires an O
on trunks of cars, antlers on the poles
conducting lightning speech. On August mornings
you heard these summer insects, locusts,
and looking past the looming cottonwoods
and over lilacs, fences, you thought
it was the sound of people talking, glowing nodes
pressed through a wire. And then at dusk
rolling homeward in some slanted light,
the landscape took on curves that had always
seemed designed, and from blue space, serene—
but closer, random, rocking with chaos,
fountaining with violence.

You have the measles, you are quarantined indoors.
You trace the metal numbers on the screen door.
Outside, in the concrete double-drive, your brother
casts a rod and reel, an arc into the dim end,
daylight savings. Your mother peels potatoes
at the sink—her lips shape soundless words.
Your sister wanders home from junior high, for lunch.
She and her girlfriend watch *Dick Van Dyke,*
a gray-white Tuesday, and eat on TV tables: tuna-fish,
potato chips. You try to get attention by tripping
on a hassock like Rob Petrie, wisecracking from the corner

of your mouth, like Morrie Amsterdam. Silence.
So you do jumping-jacks while standing in the closet,
rocking by your phonograph, its hot motor smell in plastic.
You were singing *Ferry Cross the Mersey*,
Gerry and the Pacemakers. Also Dusty Springfield,
who sang *Wishin' And Hopin'*, your favorite song.
You had glass 78's: *The Artist's Life,*
Tales from the Vienna Woods. Barnacle Bill
the Sailor. Slap Her Down Again, Pa.

What is the method, this century?
I think it is a thing ground fine,
then spread and rolled, silver, sylvan,
silent, *en grisaille,* black haloed like
the sodium lights in early video,
punching holes in the coin-colored sky.
For most of history, when history was made,
so few showed up for any large event.
Now you crouch for shadow presentations,
entranced before a box with figurines
in snub-nose pirouette, assassin finger puppets,
the big jet roaring home, black haloes
in the air around coronas, like whorls
of negativity, a chaos emblem,
a depthless eye to warn us, this
we should not penetrate, this holy
shroud of Now; don't rend the real,
this deep grimoire, bird-laced, rounded,
sunned. And then a funeral with the caissons,
horses. Drums. To go with the trumpets.
Backwards boots in stirrups. A young girl asks,
are they his boots?, stunned.

Nightly News. Chet Huntley is a dry man
smoking in the dark. He tells the booming,

flying land a story. And when he tells,
the rest areas fall silent, and pictures loom
above his shoulder. A cigarette plumes lazy
at his crooked elbone. Roll the credits,
with the *molto vivace* from Beethoven Nine,
whose sharp non-sequitur timpani thwacks
recall loopy genius, and splice us to history, Chet.
He leaves at night beneath a sloping hat,
and loping past the outdoor weatherman,
the fella with a marker and a tri-state map,
(a mix of sun and clouds) heads off to Lindy's,
for a scotch.

2

For the complicated, handsome, sickly man,
a bread-box with a flag around it.
We saw his head, that waved a flag of blood.
In autopsy photos, childhood loiters in his face.
His little boy salutes and squints, Oswald's stiff
hid underground, not a parapet to pole his head.
In five years, another brother, a fell year.
Two months prior, a great black King
lined out in a tufted coffin, dead,
draped on the back cover of *Look.*
He rolled from behind the neighbor widow's garage,
the cover snapping open in the drive.
The kitchen window curtains pull aside,
all handlessly. I imagine this, and widows
everywhere, who in infinite, separate
living rooms, lurch in crepe, from winking
TV screens to pristine, folded beds.
Lay back with your shoes on, Mother.

Your oldest brother had a girl with looming hair,
and while he drove, you sat between, a drive-in Saturday:
hardware, car wash, Wimpy's. You bumped her cigarette,
which made her nylons melt. And he, soon Air Force
classified in Bangkok, let you have it.
And figuratively then, he let them have it.
Then they let us have it. Then I let you have it.
It goes around.

3

What is the method? There were other methods.
There was mud, then stone, a little iron.
Woodland felled. Now unlike things are mixed
and ground and rolled. Materiality
is rendered first in vats. It never scents,
in any way, the trail of the sun.
Never a contour cut by time. And
there are no flaws. Our method of air
is transit. It is a material of transit. Our method
of water is no longer harness, but ubiquity.
It spirits away turds everywhere, and I mean
everywhere. You wouldn't believe
where we can *do* that! The method of ground
is ground, though there is a second ground,
a colony of the *idea* of ground,
an unmysterious lump, a myth gone to a dump, the moon.
I almost forgot we ever went, because,
and no one says it, it was dull, and not a little dull,
but fabulously so. We'll stay pent down here.
We touched goal is all. No money in it, either.

O my beautiful.
O my beautiful, again beautiful, some pitted china
pulled from a house fire's cooling nest,

a naked bed lit only by a streetlight, a face
the life has fled from. O my beautiful that was less,
there was soundless groaning that night in 1969
from three billion souls. Something
had gone out of it. That *this* is all it is,
our moon, less interesting than a desert,
less rich with surprise than an empty parking lot
in sodium light, a few millennia of fable
dashed by Neil and Buzz, athletes doing calisthenics
while you fitful sleep, or rise at four,
parched and padding to the fridge to gulp cold milk
straight from the bottle, leaning on the door
with a drastic local headache. Then,
passing through the living room, you see
the lost white wafer floating, hovering
in her stygian cricket-dark, alive
in dreaming only. You are unmaidened,
and will ever you be swan'd again or not
some distance underneath her,
your thin feet joined in the living black grass,
your thin feet painted with her, beautiful.
My beautiful, O my beautiful.
O my beauty. My dead moon.

4

Walking sidelong down the street
to present a smaller target to the world,
as though it made a difference. Which it doesn't.
She crawled backward on a car trunk for assistance
in a pink nubby-weave suit. Not that *you* knew
what this was like, picnicking by trestles.
The lake-glass quivered slightly when your line
disturbed the water, and trees spired
upside down. Fields out to a tree line

of mixed hardwoods! A wizardly oak. Arrowheads
in furrows. A cemetery with iron stars akimbo,
last century's dead mulching the earth,
unalterably virtuous, by virtue of their death.

You drove a little while, then parked and walked together
through the trees, and finally spread a blanket.
You covered her body with yours, awkwardly,
not even lustfully, and for an unknown reason,
under the watchful sky, under the tall trees,
fresh young hominids in a temperate forest,
Early Quaternary period, the Holocene Epoch.
Your girlfriend was distracted. Her soundless lips
formed words. You tripped over some roots
to get attention, faked a pratfall.
You wisecracked from the corner of your mouth
like Red Skelton.

Goodnight and God Bless.

Your life is a long strip of sky-colored film
framed with bare branches.

There, the two of you, who chase bright love
around in one another, pant together
in her bed. There you saw the two of you
from far above and from the side,
then from the other side, in rapid flashing.
Both your trains came in together, timely, timely,
but your *ka, auteur,* remained aloof,
stood by, some distance from the good thing.

Who cannot touch it.
In your house with central heating.
With your walls lined with some distant
fraction of world culture, listening to Delius,
some languid, lovely music of the swamp.
What's left of a fish is scuppered in oil
in a frying pan on the stove.
You who cannot touch it, eating a pear.
Who cannot touch it, which is grief.
Nothing, no salt in the eyes, a sigh that sounds
more bored than anything, a fantasy of houses
looming over swamps, on stilts. Solitude
among the mute and pendant leaves.
Long hammock days. You, enchanted
on the balcony, lank-haired, bearded,
frail, with a lap rug and some crackers,
reclining in a wicker chair. Beneath
the dead crusader cheekbones, death,
a sort of wildlife stalking in the lymph,
exotic and discreet. Who cannot touch it.

In the 13th century, a nun named Margery
of Kempe expressed humility before God
by incessant weeping.

But you are here, and grief approaches
from the street and up the drive. Some cars
sough by. She has a little hat with netting
hanging down, with small faux asters tangled
in the veil. Her scent is like cut flowers
and clean closets, cedar; faintly, photo chemicals,
official documents that bloom with mildew.
Her eyes blink on and off somehow,

some gradient of light behind gray irises
going through its changes; some nearly frozen birds
passing by a window, in February.
The brittle day is kindling. The tiny birds
strobe the room almost imperceptibly,
and a minor comet is thrown on the horizon,
its tail folded behind it, like a check mark
in a ledger, the morning sky the color
of an open mouth, an unlikely,
shredded looking place.

She crosses her legs. Her stockings
make a nylon whisper, and she smokes.
The smoke twines up. Some morning sparrows
commence the skirling that they do in cities,
the way they always did when you were dull-eyed,
enervated, sleepless.

But the room reddens, and rises, and glows.
The music swarms in greater tides,
ascending modulations, new lands unrolling
out from under one another to reveal
the silver brass frontier, threaded
with a golden, crawling river.
There is duration, more than change.
You don't know why. And then you say,
don't ask me why.

DUSK IN CENTRAL PARK

We're sloping home at night, the dusk above
expanding, slow, a grave, unnoticed progress.
In the full and heavy air that laves the park,
late summer insects are the only friction.
Of all known wounds, the worst are untold loves.
In dense cities we exhale them, and they open
in the air, like heat blots on a stuttering film.
A fissure bleeds in pond-glass by the bridge.
San Remo's towers have been sucked in,
the swans revolving drain bound in a knot
of fear. And look, my eyes are blotted out
or rather crossed with sets of vacant x's—
a cartoon superhero under spells
and bad enchantments. How frail
and full of air we are, who cry and fade,
implode at this black touch, undifferentiated
want, the spoor of untold love.
We could unbind each other, you and I.
There lives a fantasy we could unbind
each other, the twilight reservoir gone molten,
a Maxfield Parrish afterlife. Or not.
Instead, I'll keep revolving in my ribcage,
where I'm watching you, behind the bars.

THIS KINDLED BY GAUDE VIRGO SALUTATA, A MOTET BY JOHN DUNSTABLE, C.1400

Slow-spreading English music, as though
we watched a pale drawing-off of the night
from delicate fields, and heard a haunt
of griffins in a fog close by the house.
How one of the griffins, without fire, has wrought,
by a concentration of time, a face in gnarled elm wood
with a spell hidden in its hands: to warp, to whorl the wood,
to make water freeze and thaw and unvisibly fade,
to make fire ash, to make fire even without fire,
and carve an eddy in the air that turns his maneuver
into a major wind: kissing the barn-wood high up,
over-filling the air over the ocean,
causing a wrinkle in the salt-drift engendering thunder.
How a griffin loves with his hands the way
we walk without shoes after winter,
painfully, for the first time in a year.
But after all this is spoken of, it is the tenderness
I haven't stolen for this poem: the griffins
droning after the rain, touching the wood
to make a face in the bole of a tree, another hybrid,
one being falling into someone else.

THE MOZART D MINOR PIANO CONCERTO

Charon's oar is turning Acheron.
His rolling barge is overfilled with masquers,
freshly scarab'd, panting, off on a tear,
the fleeing flashbulb princesses and drivers,
suburban youth with massive trauma,
forever smiling stop-framed on their faces.
The agitated flocks of newly dead
bearing cedar boughs in flames, are wild
to disembark, to mount another circle,
an inversion of the one they left behind.
Standing on and on, they know
the smell of burning pine and anise,
marzipan and wax, and something louche
about it too, a scent of lately roguering
in winding sheets. Then from the open clouds,
chromatic spells of snow, astringent, sulphurous,
a match beneath the nose, and they recoil.
Cold or hot the sound, what difference does it make
to morning starlings, anyhow a new release
of reptiles, stating themes as wracked as life?
They were improvising *now* and *now,*
and only one could tame that ugly beauty,
so much fiercer written down, and lifelike,
don't you think? It has the arch tenacity of time.
It's life, the favorite hangman of the queen
caressing you to death, but with *tendresse,*
as pure and criminal as ivory. Around
the stage receding on the shore, and through
the frame of this one, cast up by the river,
it rhymes with all the sing-songs of your mother.
It resembles both of you.
It sounds like both of you so much.

MAHLER

Sweet *Ländler* of the old.
The day is not remarkable for its uniqueness, but its age.
December afternoon.
The magic visitation of the sun.
St. Anthony is preaching to the fishes,
snow on the banks thrown everywhere
like salted rags, disordered rooms of snow.
The unseen happens under water.
We should remember the fluidity of fishes,
and these, with temporary, grinning
human faces, annealed by two uplifted
fingers, sent back to swimming, joyful
in their vertigo controlled.

Songs of the West.
Famous songs and tirades of the West.
The woodsmen whistling in museums, the sky
a prison that is not a prison.
The sky as code, a referent, the empirical
a song dreamed up by angels, and intoned
by St. Martha, electricians.
All in all, the metaphysical for phones.

His symphonies,
a dwelling of the magic and the real.

In New York City, Mahler and his wife
attended seances. For then,
Theosophy was everywhere. (The government
of Costa Rica was elected on this ticket, and obsessed
with astral planes.) At one of these, a mandolin,

aloft, tapped him on the forehead.
He and his wife took days to talk it out,
the table rising, the curtains rustling.

I said to the air, *give out.*
Metaphysics are a wish for working, better hearing,
a shiver on the stairs, some wishing in the woods,
a fall in undulating einkorn, wheat knotted in your fists.

Dark forests. Stone cities. Cold rain.
His brain cuts clarinets from trees,
and he makes them plaintive with the winter pain,
where the wings of city crows snap like *rute* in the Park,
surfing on an updraft from the bitter Western ocean.
He leans over the sill of the Savoy Hotel,
over the ladies of the New York Phil,
below in phaetons, who hum polite, exalted tunes.
Meanwhile he notates menace gone to triumph,
then halfway back to the banal. The elevator man
is sampling sherry on his breaks, and croons,
And how is Mr. Mahler today? I hope
he's feeling better.

Hear a man's brain, now doubled over,
stagger through the room.
Sudden and loud, an angel snorts dead coffin air
through dusty drainpipes, and silver trains roar through the naves
of Romanesque cathedrals, and a parade that chimes is surging to the wharf
where whole regattas set their sails beneath opulent green stars.
As they surge, they're waving banners, high aloft Klimt women
with their chins held up, with parted lips, closed eyes.
Thin children with their drums, in ranks,
proceed above the fancy snow of March,
and entities awake from field and marsh
whose names have not been called in several centuries.

The special telephone is ringing at the Christian Science Building.
The other end is Mary Eddy's tomb, and should we answer?
These entities are swarming everywhere,
on roads he hiked through mountains,
by the grave of his diphtheria daughter,
on the floor of the Attersee, Salzkammergut,
his pale intrusive form seen from below.

LORCA

Gathered to his murder, he drops
a carton of assorted teeth behind
the olive trees. This is the first of many
moonless nights, the first of many slaughters.
Beneath a poem there is a poem, a voice
that wonders what has happened. Beneath a poem
there is a scream that cannot read or write.
He will look younger for a day or so.
The shadows tented underneath his eyes
decamp, then flee below the eves.

He's breathing there awhile. The teeth attend.
They quickly become bored, are soon
rethread and read in squarer languages. They only
rattled under beds in Spain like bombs
composed of chalk and moonlight. They wound
the nighttime's living spies, but leave police states
standing ashen and erect.

But in the Summerland, the Neverglades,
Federico has a new vocation. Now he
has the leisure to indulge a lifelong
passion for music. Trading in piano
and guitar, he splits from the cold, bloody
forest clarinets and oboes, a power
of bass drums. One hundred and eleven,
The Lorca Orchestra swarms the planet's rim
at dusk, far from ears and open windows.

They are expected to reach hurricane strength
tonight.

Startled and at full attention, musicians
read their fresh dispatches. Surging toward
the coastline, ten to twenty miles an hour,
humming like grasshoppers, musing together in pairs,
using the buddy system, descending at landfall.

Inadvertently they topple the smudge pots in the steaming orchards.

He's floating, who was never seen to run.
Tonight he'll lead the making of soft gyres
in farmers fields, combing down the wheat
into a whorl atop the crown of this
new planets head, which, being round, is everywhere.

THE SPIRAL MANEUVER

On a Plane from England, Leaving Behind Ravens,
and Bodies of Water with Swords In Them.

Llyn Padarn, Llanberis, Wales.

Tea colored water, stones covered
with brown furze, as though the lake
were floored with bibles, the *words of Christ in Red:*
the leatherette embossed, the blood-red letters
furring like the filters of the cigarettes
in an American or London park.

The lakes forgot their nature speech. They murmur
vaguely of their beauty, mirrored prayer.
No response from even sessile oaks
that twist through time in Gael. Only
commentaries, Methodist, on Jesus, work and drink.

The spice girls in the margins of the quarry
parking lot, teen Magdalene's with radio,
don't see me, but suddenly ignite
into some singing, old and Welsh,
three bars that make me shiver in the sun.

Lyn Llydaw

I am on the shore of a Lake
where, according to legend, Arthur's sword
was thrown. The Lady of the Lake
clutches it. In ten thousand years,

(because we are between ice ages)
the ice will slowly crowd this cym,
and when it has receded, leave the impress
of some chopper blades, steeped
in turf and slate, serrations
like the digits of the pterodactyl,
an emblem of the Age of Machines.

London Notes

London rhyming with itself.

A museum diorama of the Roman city
has pre-recorded birds
for atmosphere.
I hear the same birds later on
that day, High Holborn,
behind Fleet Street,
skirling in an utter silence.

Time is in transit in London,
in the Templar Church,
where the Earls of Pembroke,
three generations, flake
in the round knave, molecules
still sifting down the aisles
in Blitzkrieg aftershock.

On my tongue, the flavor
of molecular smoke,
the slowest possible burning in time.
Their legs are crossed, having
found a good position
for an eternity of repose,
casual, in suits of salt, anchoring Temple Bar
to the Embankment.

On the First Sunday after Ascension
the rector (returning the miracle
to the ordinary, which is the birthplace
of miracles) tells of
He who has not died,
but merely changed the mode
of His presence.

A day is an overlay.
For all I know, forms do not die,
but merely change the mode
of their presence. Walking by
Bloomsbury Square,
a rat-crossed copse near dawn,
a young man is rocking,
slowly. Another, on his knees
in front of him. The standing man
lifts up his shirt, to display
his faun-colored ass. The masks of God
are local, and does this one rhyme
with the fan-vaulted ceiling in the Abbey
by the unknown genius
who worked for Henry Tudor,
only this time by Brancusi?

What I don't know about the Thames
could fill it, but I saw the swords
drawn from its floor, steeped
in the color of the river.
They have not perished, but only
changed the mode of their presence:
sapphire on their first immersion,
then river-colored. A mystery
why the Thames is birthing scores
of swords, some, seemingly,

designed for river-throwing. One
could admire a people
that threw their swords in the river,
but they may not be the same people
who took them out.

Time is in transit in all London,
the capital of—as the Sioux called it—
Grandmother Land,
in honor of Victoria Regina, and itself
a grandmother: an old woman
with a hundred suitors in her past,
divorces and catastrophes untold,
plagues, sirens and explosions,
with mismatched plate, threadbare
antimacassars, salt on her winds
when you pass through her whalebone house,
maritime and dank, peculiar food
combined at random, pell mell, in her cupboards.
She owns a set of ravens at the Tower,
the most arrogant birds on earth.

One may light anywhere on the
Spiral, which is time. Holy Saturday
was a good place, when the tabernacle was
empty, and the heart of the matter,
as usual, obscured. I remember
the scent of vinegar for the painted eggs,
what was latent in the sponge
hoisted to His lips. That is the first
overlay. There is a truth to tell, that
the heart of the matter is absent,
and my heart also, another overlay.
I see tokens of love in unlikely places,
but wage war on onlookers. Another

sweaty hominid in silks, it is dangerous
to speculate on my chances for happiness
to my face. The heart attends, gasping,
in an air pocket, and hence the imperative
for poems, for mounting the spiral
to begin, wherever.

The entire universe is happening
in each electron of each atom.

The actuality of the past may
be recovered by indirection,
as new planets that cannot be seen
may be recovered by the carom
of light rays from their parent suns,
aimed from a distance.
Also, the magnetic field is sensitive,
a membrane I may touch at one end,
to shake loose some hidden lover
at another. Put your hand in where
my heart was, here. Recover my heart
by indirection. If I can see
whom my unseen heart revolves around,
could I vault a poem, glancing from
those absences, to locate a presence?

There is no *over there,*
or *back there,* which is where
I got the spiral. How last Tuesday
rhymes with the same day
in 1124, because the moment
is adjacent, contiguous to the other
on a clear, winding helix of days.
And last Tuesday is just as unrecoverable

as 1869, and so not further removed,
one day not more *vanished*
than another.

In Sarajevo, children try their feet
in Princips' concrete shoes, the way
tourists try their hands in film stars'
handprints in New York.
The past is not *over there,*
but sits astride the present
and within it, in concentric circles:
not just a spiral, but a helix in depth,
world within a world.
The cosmos bequeathed to us
was invented before geology,
the telegraph, the telephone,
hypnosis. Our picture of the cosmos
was made before the advent
of the human marvelous.
But there were shells, there were cicadas,
and thin sheets printed with change
in geologic beds. There was always
overlay. By indirection,
I may locate myself in this,
some tortile dancing—
my Seven Souls perched on the helix
at divers points, waiting
to be plotted out, in outline,
like Arcturus bleeding through
or the Green Man in the vaulting,
Aphrodite teeming in his teeth.

Time is in transit, and it only slows
where it is cradled in one
consciousness, slowed to a crawl

by language, which might
be its purpose: to fix the world
for examination, to still
the sides of the whirling
centrifuge, to note the way rivers,
lakes and gods cradle time,
and nurse eventualities.

Time is in transit by my eyes.
Estuaries channel near them, like
deltas shot from the air.
I have worked to change
the mode of my presence,
and to write this poem
merely as a track, a sign
that I was here, to work my deviled face
onto the ceiling of the cloister
of the frieze at Canterbury,
where Becket entered to become another:
one among six billion in the progress
of a short-lived race still in its youth,
and, like all youths, enchanted
by the poignancy of refusal.
But those spells, and youth, are done.

TRAIN

Illinois, the green sea sleeping. Chicago papers
rustling at our feet, turning brown with age in fifty miles.

They tell us what a violent land we live in, but this train
is like a laundromat on wheels, the same benign code

of looking, and looking away. I am held captive as a shirt,
tumbling. One could almost learn to like this long, sweet

grieving of the nothing to be done. Pairs of eyes
are watching as I saunter to the club-car for one more

tin-canned Margarita. Across the aisle, two young married
Parsis, immaculate in white, are folded one into the other

with two red suns between them, one burning on each forehead.
Do you remember that they slept for almost fourteen hours

or maybe one whole day between them, two suns on either side?
They were still sleeping early afternoon next afternoon

when Europeans and other thin white cranes finally dipped
their beaks between the kudzu leaves and up from *Kreuzwort Rätseln,*

and outside people left their cars to watch the train pass by,
airless and sufficient, float past their houses, down Mrs. Ippy's

thigh, down to the Bloodflower, where Tennessee wrote plays,
watched boys, sold mammy dolls and postcards in fluorescent

morgue light on St. Peter. Meanwhile, the tracks were curving.
I saw the moon first *there,* then there, then over there, and then

the red roads gray with tarmac, two colors merging like the color
of a brain, that is, a thing irremediably polite paved over

something seething, something raw, something hidden in a wave
or a handshake, in a kiss. And you were sleeping too, with your

flying gift for regular oblivion, mouth slightly open,
plaits like garden snakes stealing down your brow, waking, looking out

long after midnight at gritty downtown Memphis, an exhausted movie set.
And then you slept again, and then it grew so strange to haunt the sleeping

train, lights haloed and horrific in the glass, infants tossed like casualties
on their mothers, lovers on each other, and even bored night porters nodding,

novels whispering on their knees. I couldn't hear or smell outside, where black leaves
gusted toneless in the wind, plangent maybe, under railroad bridges, over

rivers we kept crossing. No, the same river: stars in left hand glass,
heat lightning in the right.

ONE AFTERNOON

One afternoon—and it was June, I think,
I asked to fall asleep beneath her skirts,
and she consented, this while
sitting at piano, pounding out
some piece by Gluck. And it was green
like China, with sunlight shining through—
green like China, and warm there while she sang,
her booted foot that smelled like earth
pumping the brass piano pedal.
And it was green like China,
and we drank china tea.
And there was Gluck. I think it was
The Dance of the Spirits.
It made me curious about her, that she
consented thus, to let me sit under her skirts
where it was green like China.

And out the window, the Michigan
birds sang, but all day we were in China,
as in a play, or a tableau, of China.
And then she brought some beer, and
shuffled toward me, and we bowed
politely to each other, nipped from the pail,
and we were Chinamen.

And then we saddled Chinese horses,
little horses, and rode off to the Lake, which was
the China Sea. The Lake was green,
with jesting waves. Dead alewives,
which were Chinese carp, were glinting
in the old sun going down

to China.
She said she'd like to wash her hair,
and she did this, by simply diving in, and
then she let it dry out on my face, as I had
requested. I lit my smoke.
The match was blue, the color of a gas flame.
And I nearly fell asleep there, without hope—
not hopelessness—there is a difference.
We did not want to leave.
Pulsing, dry hands together, green colors
coming down, *bloodboatcolorloftinglife.*
Terrifying peace.

FELL SUMMER

The day was fell: so hot, and monthly blood for her.
Myself, one-eyed and snappish, having torn a lens.
A plague of deer flies on the beach, and then, at dusk,
a yellow storm spit needles on the porch.

We fled inside to argue, where the curtains planed
above the bed. The light was spectral. I don't
remember much of what was said. We were
looking at each other, and talking to ourselves.

I drove her to her work, three dozen bright miles south.
The sky was blue and heedless, and if something evil
happened there, she wouldn't say. In secrets,
love is circumscribed. The distances are catching fire,

the copper fuses in the handset when I call.
I won't turn on the lights. I'll let the house
roll into darkness in its own surround of dark,
hold to my nose the swelled night-ripening

tomatoes we put in; pacing, smoking, seeking out
some level on this silver, black-delineated rail.
Further down the curve, she stumbles when she sees
her portion of the night that shudders down

and masses in the wood. There is nothing
I can do. I think she sees the living daylights
being turned out of the trees. Sometimes the darkness
walks, sometimes it hurtles through the leaves.

Notes from the Summerland

The distant
and the dead: for both we
have been asked to swear to certain
things. Your distances are facts. East, over the
curves, you hide in the land. Where absence comes and
is let in, there you will be carved out: a frieze of
mantes on the bole of an elm, praying in
green cabinets, sudden moths
on a white wall in
winter.

Other
than that distance is
the riddle common to both
realms, I do not know what I hope to gain
pretending to be one of you, pulling off this mask so
light it is an act of faith to wear it, to go where I am not up or down,
to the right or to the left. I divide it with my hand,
that place and this, a gesturer, parting the
the colors in some dim
cartoon where these
things might be
known.

Birds
change plumage
in midair, and everyday
the sky is born in a new place.
Another tent for the walkers, rolled out
for the sleepers and the screamers. You pass
under it, asleep and laughing, hold an icon. We do
not know him. But there is your uncle, playing whist.
He makes his heaven like a pile of clean laundry,
banked with clouds. He bends down to your aunt,
heliotropism in reverse. She irons, irons,
vertical and nervous. Insubstantial
feet creep through
the blinds.

I,
a bad
loser, finally
taking the body of a
wild boar, grunt before you, drunk on
wild roads. Under your boyfriend's engine
I use my horns to spoil a pleasure trip. Lights go on
at the inn. You bathe and light each other's cigarettes, and
talk of art and other spooks. This way I see so little;
the shadow of your umbrella, the ghost of
the notebook you write in. Two
dim lights waver
awake.

Signal
to me. I will turn
in mid-sleep, and whirl to
you: a small slipstream, an over-tow,
braiding the top of your hair, passing smoke-
hands through your before and after, a mirage in the road
of rainwater fit to drown in. An airplane flies through me.
I think of astral planes, stay safely on the lower.
I wait to move again. Things I left
unfinished, detain
me.

TEMPLATE

Tonight, I fear that where my heart was
the whole thing wavers faintly
on a template: a broadcast of error and tenderness,
a scrim of loss with planes pinned on it,
clear days run through with sound: the locusts
a green line through middle air,
and peeling sycamores over the dry street,
draped on one another, lepers never coupling.
This template is as sleepless as I,
fading when I fade, fixed and staring
at the last, a kaleidoscope
someone has let go of, disremembered
on a sill, shards fusing in the sun.

This is to say that, when the eclipse
resolves, the dancers stop, and look up.

Much of what shows there will
never be known. Before this eclipse,
and cast on this template mostly Absences
breathe on, fogged on this platen where
the breath blooms and shrinks, a trace.
Myself.

THE WRONG SORT OF CHALLENGE

Inspired, in part, by Pierre Vidal, troubadour

The notion that my mistakes represent some kind of wisdom
is the wrong sort of challenge. After three million years,
that I might be expected to be excited by less than starvation,
or knives, or advancing in a line red-jacketed
while visible lead churns the air, or my blood splashes and sizzles
on a green-wood pyre, is not realistic. That my libido
would be immediately gratified, and that, if not,
I might have recourse to some retribution,
or at least shout at the party in question, is not acceptable, either.
That I should nod sagely and demonstrate my patience,
my devotion, has only been acceptable since the troubadours,
but I'd rather be a failed troubadour, like that sucker
arm in arm down Clinton street, bringing home takeout
and Lester Young, to ordinary smells, a futon with cat hair, and her.
This is how other men come to seem like princes,
while I dress in a wolf pelt, and am beaten by shepherds on the Q train,
because her emblem is the *wolf*.
And never, since the age of twelve, have I abandoned the notion
that drawing a saber and leading a charge
is the right sort of challenge, and I hated chess
because there is no room for saber charges. Some people
think I'm clever but I'm not, and I hate cleverness
because it's the wrong sort of challenge, though I suspect
if the crops were failing and I needed to be a teamster again,
needed to be a teamster again though my team was lame,
this might be a challenge that would make more sense to me,
if maybe more hopeless, which makes sense, also.
And you, of all people, should understand this,
for I, who would give you everything you asked for,
represent the wrong sort of challenge, since the right
sort of challenge would be someone who turns around

and comes back to get you, where you wait in the dark,
and who had never done this yet, and who you would wait for,
forever, to perform this task, which is my fantasy also.
All of which makes you, sadly, the right sort of challenge, for me.

VIRGIL'D

Who have wounded, have also virgil'd me,
have shown me hells, their hells or mine,
as though they walked me to a square inside a church
from which small vantage the illusion
of endless disappointment is supposed
to come out right: a tumbling frieze
of disappointments, a rain of falling horses
on the ceiling, writhing, in vanishing-point perspective.
But I'll be gone before they finish ghosting
to the tile, to my home places, necessary
or not, wholly reactive, or not:
a place of slowly rivers and thin chimes,
a rolling land returning to itself, and elms.
The gnarled stump fences hum at roadside
and I say they are alive, with long, sad
faces, Romanesque, slow moving in the grain,
their hair and beards cut deep and waving
like every mournful Jeremiah, and stones,
whole as an untold secret, holding fast a world
where all the disappointments have been known
already, and whose beauties come again.

A DREAM OF OLD TOYS

When I was small, I had a dream of a room under a room,
a basement under the fruit cellar, the hatch drifted with pink sand.
And under the hatch, the room sloped dark, like the room above it,
and it smelled like mildew, and myrrh.
And in that room were wooden boxes of old toys.
The boxes were dun-colored, and had been painted many times.
And I didn't know the toys, or rather I remembered them,
or remembered remembering them, and what was in the boxes I can only guess:
old redcoats crossed with the emblem of the Duke of Marlborough,
sea life, calcified and spiny to he touch,
and starfish come alive again in new water;
a Huguenot rood cut from marsh briar,
shawls fine enough to be drawn through an amber thumb ring,
and daggers chased with goddesses and insects.
And in another box, maybe just as I'd left them,
a glory of my first toys, augmented,
this time with the power of speech.

Starfish, you are a Peer of the Realm.
This room is for all of you, it's yours, and you've one of your own,
at the back of the closet, behind the clothes you won't wear,
and it cannot be breached by another, or the contents purloined by the Vatican.
At the top of the checkered stairs curving back to yourself
is a box with an enameled painting of you, a triptych of old lives.
The first panel is called *Mounting a Wooded Hill in Gaul,*
where you climb a hill to the hollow sound of rolling acorns.
The second is called *Fording the Severn,* and you wade across
to a droning of rebecs and the music of harness.
And in the third panel, you are spiraled there
Curled in Cool Ferns After the Soothsayer Touched You,
monitored by fireflies, where once again you sleep.

CICADA

1

Even before the story begins, you endure
a hundred subtractions not accounted for
in this turning: a grimness coming down
that doesn't answer to your name, and wayward
urgencies of memory that have you stupefied,
engrossed. I'm thinking you don't know
how much. What do you know of it,
your spectral, green, small icehouse wound,
and under it, the wounds of others, owned
by a line of hominids with lips compressed,
concealing mossy teeth, and in the DNA,
a quiver of time defying ecstasies and ailments
gone underground for thirteen generations,
like cicadas, only to surface in you?

No fewer, and I'm thinking you don't know
how many, there are obscure enchantments
knotted in your nerves. Atavistic old religions
shoal at night, in choirs, in silent tides,
on highways driving after dark, cornball
music on the radio fading in and out,
mile markers signaling.
Your passengers asleep, you wouldn't tell
them anyway, how the willow, the willow
in the margin of the road, closes
its eyes, in its winter branches feels
the glamour of the sea, and whatnot.
Now, these drooping trees possess you
with sensations you call love.

But as a wavering kid, both you and I
were scared of willows. I saw you running
only halfway down a neighbor's drive
because a giant willow loomed there,
whispering, distracting, a restless cover.

My traces all over your life but I don't say a word.
Can't write a word but to say *hello,*
and not even that. I speak to you, silent-like,
and I speak over your shoulder.
Well, I *am* you, and also
your last turning, the last of many who have
writhed and sweated, bled, gone loose and joyful
since we walked erect. I'm thinking
I don't know how many. A long blurred
picture show, in color. A snake of selves,
of men, of women. A reach. A million years.

When I lived, the unseen had me in a passion:
the inside of the cupboard when the door is closed,
and not just table rapping, ouija boards
(*Hello .... Good-bye*)
or only pieces we remember, but the
whole past. Unverifiable statistic.
How many dead were ever planted
in the earth? Now I've some idea of things
connected, so I lower a sounding into your world,
where you hear one voice, not useful for anything,
stretched out over imponderables, like sheetwater,
like creekglass over fossils. We'll be
a recording instrument of an unknown type,
a bespoke wheelbarrow piano made of bark,
sensitive, picking up the thin, high
music of age, the rainwater, sap and blood
voice of the gone away, here and braided

in gutters. We'll trundle it down the garbage-
strewn creek-bed wearing specially designed
poplar leaf headphones.
It'll be made of brown bottle glass and bark,
sandstone with sheet music pressed in it,
poems in a lava book. We'll be conductor
and operator, green and pared down
like a walking stick, a praying mantis.
I'll pass the instrument over the creek-bed,
holding the ear trumpet wired with a vine
over to an old ringer washer
owned by the grandnephew of a cousin's grandmother's
great good goddamn granddaughter who saw
you on the street and didn't know who you were—
then over to an old gin bottle, over to a sparrow,
over to you, seventy-eight inches of remembering,
rhapsodic.

2

Your passengers asleep, you wouldn't voice
your genuine suspicion that nothing is dead,
nothing is really dead. Not your father,
not your brother: seraphs, larvae,
hooded Saracens who pod in glowing mail,
in breastplates woven of small chains,
who recommence inside you
in these odd approximations of themselves,
the breastplate glinting, a knotted snake there regnant,
describing absence, but signifying the whole.

Remember how your father
built the fountain in the yard? It wasn't
grounded well. Remember how you liked
to sink your arm in there? All your bones

would sing in milky white polyphony,
an osteocantata. But it slayed
the starlings. Summer evenings you would
find one floating there, smoothly planed and
rounded, flash-totemed at the moment of its death.

The starling is your body.

The greater part is on to other singing,
the chrysalis discarded.

Between the two of us, we are the agitated
ghosts from nowhere, adhering, but obscured,
like mantes on the boles of willows.
New incarnations, or the genome, as you please,
we are a multiple of selves, myself gone just before,
the whisperer, the train man.
As below the willow, all our pasts are huddled,
fearful or malign, at taproot.
I know you, and I've seen the way you pod
in your own skeleton, a larva, once again incarnate.
Our totems are the same:
cyclones, bats and effigies on tombs,
the emblem Oroborus; cicadas, willows,
woodknots, whorls of every kind,
and portraits of the hurricanes, time-lapsed
from upper atmospheres:
Alpha, Buster, Cleo, Diamond Jim.

Vortices. One night you had a dream:
a tornado in your neighborhood burst
from behind the willow, from the south-southwest.
Green and white and livid, an intelligence,
it churned the trailer parks, but seemed
to follow ancient stitches in the ground

as though tracing veins of amber, or of
water, or of magnetism. It stopped
before your house, not knowing where to go,
like a horse that patiently awaits instructions.

Another night, not long ago, in summer,
you saw me on the white road by the lake.
I swayed a little in a cloud of fireflies,
crickets in my hat band, and traces of green fire
at collar, cuffs.
My wife, she saw me also, after I had died.
The others said she *dreamed* she saw me.
Either way, the quiet man came in again, and she said
oh!, and also, *Eldridge!* And the disappointed
light came through the glass, as if manufactured
for hotel rooms by the overpass, and near the railyards.
I glinted there a minute. Faintly,
ostinato voices came from down the hall.
She was spindly and lone looking, my Lilia
in the Taft Hotel, sitting on the bed.
She had her hanky in her right hand,
her glasses in the left. Shirt
buttoned to the top, and bowlered,
I stood there in my good black shoes
that prayed together on the tiles.
My watch fob ghosted back and forth.
Behind me, on the wall, that picture
that I bought her, *Jesus Wept,*
a print in monochrome.

I 've had a thousand endearments for her,
my willow-wood, or, *my little pasque-flower.*

When she was young, she had these boxy feet,
sunburned, dusty, a rind of callous at the heel,

and I won't soon forget her silences, like an air mass
from the arctic. Whatever room she sat in
became a northern field, where she farmed silences.

3

And nothing is dead, nothing is really dead.
I had a look-see at a news sheet yesterday.
It said there that the image of our late beloved
Chester Allan, er..uh, Garfield, *whatshisname,*
the President just kilt not long ago,
appeared transfigured in the heavens over
Talbot, Delaware.
I don't know what to believe, anymore.
More likely he is doing sleep tricks, semaphores
on stairwells in the White House, like the others
in a dance of beasts on a flooring
of dead oak trees, a chivaree. Do you know
from chivarees? It's what we used to do
when a couple would be married, stand
around the farmhouse all night long and sing,
and bang the pots and pans.

You've heard the dead on phonographs.
As surely as they live again by magnetic sorcery,
they bang the pots and pans outside
your lit-up window, and you can't hear a thing.
You, and all the others, living in this present,
at times you're like buck Mormons,
black and hunched up in yourselves,
addled by forgotten knowledge, riddles,
the invasion of free elements from every lifetime.
Your consciousness, it wheels about,
a sidelong hotel lobby waltz by Charlie Ives,
but sometimes dissonant and fresh, these sudden

leaping chords, these emblems and these totems,
like fishes bounding up from braided water.

Yours truly, when I walked here, well,
I liked the mail, and stamps, and making soup.
My brothers and myself, we liked to stand
together on the gray and red linoleum
in the kitchen, boiling soup. Northern Michigan.
February light. Suspendered, small,
mustachioed, we gripped paring knives and roots.
Our hands were white and red. We had a saying
regarding our small stature. We said,
We may be little, but Oh My!, and then we
laughed, the kettles steamed, and with bronze fire
lovely in our cracked, white china cups,
the long lush swells of future disappointment,
Christ!, seemed almost an *adventure.*

I kept a little book, and I noted down
the sounds of far off trains through different kinds
of leaves. One strain, the sound that's dopplaring
through oak, another through white pine, and so on.

4

Even before the story begins,
these urgencies of memory..........

*

I guess when the wind moves through these pine boughs, it is a sound lost
sounding as any. Nothing looks less lost than an old white pine or more lost
than a store built from it. It dangles a Nehi sign, a screen door with a bell on
it, and smells like a million stores. Empty of stock now, the owner has been
known to plain leave it unlocked and untended, such that you could filch

some postcards of deer and snowdrifts, an old brown photograph, a katydid loaded with enormous trees, the boles facing out like big cigarettes. Men in vests stand on top with bowlers, slouch hats, watch fobs, shirts buttoned to the top, no tie. In a junction like this you see one of them sleeping, that one of them is me. Run a forefinger and thumb clear round this arm; it's been the other end of a long-sleeved shirt since someone heard me talk, hunched up in my soft clothes: shame, forgotten knowledge of leaf-spattered, whirling railroad cuts, noisome shanties, firefly nights in junctions. There was whiskey and beer, singing three days and nights, eating dinner blurred and hot and loosing it in a rush, and singing some more after that. When you're alone, you imagine your colleagues with you still. My hobbies: the sound of different trains far off through varieties of leaves. Say you have there your Pere Marquette Railroad, one kind of hoot through hardwoods, another through the white pine forest, another by the dunes cold and soft in blue moonlight and a mess of crazy wheeling green stars. My my, the air is fresh with woodsmoke, just a little, the smell of the Lake like bleach, snake grass and the wet woods, also. What we ate were sardines and canned beans, you know, beans in syrup with bacon fat, and fruit maybe if it's the right time of year—a lot there for the leaving of the road for it. Find your way to fish fry if you can, walleye, all you can eat and in the wintertime smelt. After a bender it is always good if you can find provender substantial, biscuits in sausage gravy. Strong drink has always made me hungry whether my stomach wanted it or *no*. Give a Michigan shanty-boy whiskey and nothing goes wrong. One can hope my matches are not ruined with laying in the damp sand by the Big Lake, and my smokes are wadded in my shirt pocket. It just might be possible to find one that 'tisn't broke. Lilia I married when she was fourteen. I was twenty-six and going bent. She had dirty feet and was sun and snow blind, looking out bad window-glass, boxed up all winter with her younger brothers and sisters while her Dad cut timber in Missaukee. She was waiting in Buttersville—the dunes have swallowed it up nowadays. What can I do? I am small, but with a good serviceable back, my hair can be moved back with my hand. My parts are washable. I am small but shaped good: hands, legs, male parts. Already April, I fall somewheres in the near warm chill, now light after supper, yelling, the wooden town tumbling around me in an imaginary fistfight of the air.

*

Like a turning, prior to that, in which
again, again compassion for myself
and others failed, where in the town
I tumbled under veils, recessed.
Then I fled the town, and trailed behind
some ropy, lucent blood, the sputum
of the dead. I hunkered motionless
at taproot. I breathed behind the tree line
back from the road, the streaked, high cirrus
windless, cool air astringent with the pines,
a faded blue sky, plaintive.
Dusk.

I rang like a middle-sized glass bell.

I rocked down over ground, as leaves do.

Someone told the others where I was.

My mind was trilling at the south end
of the garden, where tall stalks were blowing.
And they came scything, who tore, who tore into it,
who tore. And I lived for most of it,
and not as bad as you may think, being *in* it,
the clothes of said body stretching
with the spill, the wrack, myself going slack
and flippant, mind you, and this on many themes.
On the subject of desire.
On the world of pain it lives in.
On insensate longing. On the way
a fragment wakens us, reminded,
some inside radiance released.

In another turning, long ago,
remember how you talked in firelight,
you and your brother? It was the night
the moon went out. It disappeared
only halfway through its passage.
Bats strangely circled torches, frantic.
And for once you chose to wait,
sit this one out, catastrophe again, again.
But some went mad and pounced, lawless,
threat everywhere, because all the women
would be barren, and we'd lose the blood and purpose.
The father slept, his glaive likewise asleep.
Someone old had heard this happened once before,
but had no words about it.

*

Virtual remembering.
The way the lunch horn at your high school
made you recall the screaming horn at Poitiers,
where the king wore golden bees sewn on his tunic,
and knelt before the rood,
someone splayed on branches lashed together.

*

Remember how you carved the twisted Jeremiah
who roosts on the trumeau, at the cathedral in Moissac;
who adheres there like a mantis, a water root, his beard
a sprouting plume of smoke, while from the inside,
prophetic fire consumes his long, burned scarab of a body?

In 1669, you untied her bodice
and released her breasts.
Moths flitted, throwing shadows as they hovered
by the light box near the bed,
the one she carried down the hall,
hair loosed, her feet black on the bottom.
Griselda. And she smelled wonderful,
her belly, the warm smooth salt of it,
and her armpits, slightly rank, her small, red mouth
that smelt some little of milk, and wine.
We raised up and moaned together,
our tongues entwined like snakes in combat,
while the fish hatcheries under the Louvre bubbled serene,
and plane leaves circled on the flagstones in the courtyard.

Stand by the lamp Griselda
Don't stand by the lamp Griselda
I want to stay sightless Griselda
I need to see all of you Griselda
I need to see some of you Griselda
I want to see you but only at night Griselda
I can see more of you in the dark Griselda
I have no pockmarks Griselda
Trust me Griselda
Blow the lamp out Griselda
Please play the clavier Griselda
You must know something by heart Griselda

*

It is all a world
behind a world, behind a world.

Your brother writhing on a softball field
in grande mal seizure, swimming across the lake,
a family taut with fear left on the shore.
Another brother with milked over
eyes from cataracts, scant a chromosome.
The little girl next door had mocked his habits,
his waving of his hands, and so you shoved
her head against a cupboard door. Then,
and you cannot forget this, you slapped him once
when he kicked you, the look of hurt surprise.
Once you caught him staring out the window.
The stillness was rare, his attention, unexpected.
Your greatest fear was that behind appearances,
he saw and felt all that there was to feel
and was marooned inside himself.

Ann Arbor, where all the ordinary, white frame
houses were bathed in a luminous grid. Nights.
Of rich electrical terrors. Fungi dried to potency,
like the discard of the locust. The night
the floor-length mirror in Demetrius' apartment
tipped and shattered, and you forgot who you were,
(which means you must have known, sometime)
words like *brother, mother, girlfriend,*
emblems only. A void, a vortex of utter absence,
all the aloneness that you feared for others.

But just prior to that, hallucinations,
this only when you closed your eyes,
of such surpassing gorgeousness and mystery
you still cannot believe it:
out of blackness, tomb figures, called *gisants,*
each detailed in fluorescent bronze,
men and women, armored and in chain mail,
each one different from the last.

Opening your eyes, it stopped, but closed,
they surfaced from a velvet blackness,
from either side, one before another,
as though captured on a film, shown
on an old projector. Dim footage
of a bat unfurling, an owl spreading,
a stain with the fixed fetal eye
gently rolling in the bones,
a pageant of infinite gold tenderness:
souls, each various, high-gothic, with finials and turrets,
an x-ray of a mantis, an effigy rekindling,
the details bright with the inside glimmer of bone,
as deep as a Mandelbrot Set.

To vibrate, to shatter, to be far, far away.
Music you were seeking out, the ice
you broke to wash.

I saw you with a *esclopette* in 1673,
a Flanders sunset tinting powder smoke and fire,
massed woodwinds skirling over savage drums,
and later, in your high shoes with a tennis racket,
peruk'd and languid, all in lace.

I saw you in a parade,
your head like a baby, wearing a fez
in a little Shriner's car.

I saw you bear one corner of a palette,
a slave, sacrificed with a virgin in the Lake
of the Small Voices, while Tacitus took notes.

I remember your tiresome piety.
I remember the forgivable needs that caused
you pain, and that anyone would understand,

also what you loved about yourself
that wasn't always understood.

I remember our hunger for what is limitless
beyond approximation.
Our being, all expectation, riding a bike,
standing on the petals up, up over the hill.

5

What was the husk called, and by how many names,
in large black shoes, brown hands in his pockets,
in the overexposed street, with that quiet
way of standing? The way he looks down.
The way his veins cross, wrist-wise.
Absurdly unassuming. A tree-lover,
a lover of the gnarled and the arcane,
drawn from the trees to the musick'd clearing
by any odd knot of woodwinds.

Voices just under hearing excite him,
who is prey to insensate loves. A tosspot,
ghosting through centuries, watching you,
then dying, then reborn to watch you again;
now and then hung by the neck or stretched
on the rack for buggery, for poaching,
for loitering in fields by chiming poplars
shaking shiny-side out, his camp smoke
rising near the close-willowed river.
Those willows,
their sashay, faintly...*disreputable.*

This Lazarine, with his old hat.
Who would not be caught dead
suspended roodwise. Who vanishes,

folding into heat waves in the turning road.
She's gone, her husk cast down just anywhere,
her shoes turning up at the market, his box
of trinkets at the curb, a drift of knives
to eager boys, and one small spoon, a souvenir,
and tiny coins in nearby foreign currencies.
An ordinary conch is letting out the sea,
a moment in the history of surf.

6

I don't know that I'll be going.
I don't know that it would be healthful, or prudent,
again silver the rain with the green willow waving,
all as it once was and may be again,
as was laid down once and will bear the overlay,
as can be seen through clear to the bottom,
and it doesn't matter much because in any case
I don't know that I'll be going.
I don't know that it would be healthful, or prudent,
or that I wish to be so soon specific
and away from latency.

And if I go early, I may be too soon, and rathe,
and be birthed by my own grandmother.
And if I go too late, I may be birthed
in a boarded house with a dry well
and a stunted pear tree.

I don't know that I'll be going,
so conscious that through my head streams daylight.
I don't know that I'll be going
down a long corridor to a dim, colored aspect,
the bare legs running in the park-like spaces,
and the cars running also, and the planes coming out,

and the fresh sadnesses like grass.
(O my Hyacinthus killed by a frisbee,
felled behind the Ford.)
And if I go, and if I go to stay,
one other thing I'll ask for: a hushed life,
between the wars, to haunt the slopes on wooded hills,
to summer my legs in chill, delaying rivers,
while the body thins and dries,
the faintest smell of wood smoke.
Calling, and at different depths, cicadas
scatter motionless on boles, the sycamore,
the oak; a magic spiral in the fervid,
liquid skiagraphia of leaves,
scarabs in a vortex, set like a green-star pattern.
A rattle for the infant Lazarus.

7

Ten o'clock one morning, while your mother ironed,
we gathered at the window in alarm
to hear a *Test of the Emergency Broadcast System*
on her Sears and Roebuck Silvertone Trimline Radio
which she won at a movie-house contest.
Quite a program.
A keening, long high tone, sustained.
All our Selves lined up at windowsill,
our young-old faces dopplaring behind us,
damned scared.
There is no measure of our reverence
for this lovely shitwheel.
But the world we reckon on, this day *today*...
Once, in a railroad cut near Terre Haute,
I nodded to it, evenly,
then ate more beans, and read the funnies,
and gladly sidled along, up curving roads.

I'll own to an attachment just to what endures:
the land that stretched off thisaway,
flat and crossed with fences, wires for telegraph,
and wood-lots here and there to sleep in;
orchards where deer pull apples from the trees,
and towns where firemen play baseball in the street.

New York City. Monday morning. A helicopter
wheels, then dips in the descent,
as though tracing winter birds from twenty centuries ago.
The radiator drips, and dishes turtle
in the cloudy sink. The sheltering of yourself,
it is a graceless task, white-knuckled.
Take a quarter turn.
Tie your shoes before the window.
There is the shoal of the dawn, unlikely,
and though seen a million times, somewhat unexpected;
a soprano, banked to her knees in the surf of running snow,
a stone bird kindled from within.
So beautiful, but seemingly
you cannot get inside it.
Turning after turning, it eludes you.
What you learn, you learn by long, slow processes,
like glaciers that seem not to move at all,
and then, one lifetime, suddenly
arrive.

Your passengers asleep, you wouldn't tell them anyway...
(What *could* you tell them, here and now, guiding
their splayed forms that pod in plunging metal.)
Slow breathing is a creed that demonstrates
how they yield to the integrity of the vessel,
its captaincy presumed. You wouldn't tell them anyway,
how the myth of discrete forms, and purity,
unmixed qualities, has waned with every turning,

until the notion passed forever,
a flurry of cottonwood on the brown river.
That which has no alloy is an empty bed,
a chivaree to no purpose.

The inside and the outside are the same.

Flesh is wedded to the unseen.

Unlikes haunt each other.

Love, disguised, is beautifully mishandled in the world.

Do you remember how on pilgrimage this day, sixth century,
you bought the femur of a saint?
You pestled it with mead and drank it for a flush of grace,
then sank in filthy straw. You rose long after dark
and at the portal of the church,
you saw the wolves in torchlight, sliding comic on the ice,
hindquarters twined in frozen quirts,
ravening princes of the blood in the sleeping town.

Six on the one hand,
one-half dozen on the other...

When I was young, two girls were swimming in a pond
whilst I was working hard.
They started screaming, as though drowning,
horrible screams. As I ran, I stripped
my shirt and pants off, and dove in.
When I come up, they're laughing.

We wanted you to come in!, they said.
We thought it was the only way to get you in!

I told your sister to cheer up once.

I said to her husband, *don't leave your hoe*
in the long grass where the children are playing
What time is it Mr. Fox?, and whatnot.
The Chinese elm is goal.

There's a plane, away high up.

The playground used to be a swamp.
Look at the fine grains on the ground
that hold the water still, and *yet.*

By God your boy's ears are big.
Looks like a radio.
Hair smells like leaf smoke.
He hears the furnace going on and off
at night when everyone's asleep.
And your daughter,
where'd she get that low voice, like a basset clarinet?

You only misplaced a few rocks, tossing them
into the green lake, where like as not
they'll stay, forever.
You watch the horsetail in the sky.
You bend the grass like deer.
You watch the movement in the rabbit hutches,
and white sheets on the clothesline
planing level in blue air.

A pie cools on the sill.

I saw you being laid down on a huge
white bedspread, as sailboats turned
on silver water in the sun.

I saw your mother wash you in the sink
to spare her back.

I saw you picking mulberries from the tree
across the street.

I saw you on a trike, maples swaying
over the driveway, holding yourself.
I saw you swinging on the swing,
and jumping off. It was Memorial Day.
You got up to be with Dad as he
interred petunias.
We were present there, and we remember how
a tenderness unlooked for, it rises in the road
we travel down a hundred times.
We leave again, and when alone,
it doesn't matter anyway. Our angel
double whistles in the tree, and turns us
with a wind. We follow every command,
like leaves.

PROGNOSTICATIONS

There is only this: some good will happen
in this life, with a salting of terror, but anyone
could have foretold that from the long foreground.
I would study how to please you with, say,
divination by thunder, but thunder is rare
and in the end I advance with ordinary unseeing.
I summon only the gnarled entity inside words,
surging like a vine, or congealing like stirred stone
in some mysterious, cold liquefaction, a painting
of a vast typhoon captured from space.
A schemata of this storm or of a text
might reveal a face of white fire
beneath the frozen surface of a pond.
I, strictly speaking, know your love
as I know a light rain, but I could drown
in the breakers where the world reflects itself.
This is what I have.
Run your hands over the grain of the text
where the entity gathers, massing, a green sun-wraith
growing from a wound. The wound
describes a whorl, and the whorl describes a hope
on the other side of blessing.

POEMS ON CD

AEE-5138